A MOHAWK CHILDHOOD

GROWING UP WHERE THE PARTRIDGE DRUMS ITS WINGS

Karen Gravelle

Photographs by Stephen R. Poole

GROWING UP IN AMERICA

Franklin Watts

A Division of Grolier Publishing
New York London Hong Kong Sydney
Danbury, Connecticut

> ## Dedication
> To Rachael and Strawberry,
> For helping me to see the light.
> S.P.

Cover and Interior design by Molly Heron
Map by Joe LeMonnier
Photograph p.7 ©Ron Spumer/Visuals Unlimited.
All other Photographs © Stephen R. Poole

Library of Congress Cataloging-in-Publication Data

Gravelle, Karen.
Growing up— where the partridge drums its wings / by Karen Gravelle : photos by
Stephen R. Poole.
     p.   cm. — (Growing up in America)
Includes bibliographical references and index.

ISBN 0-531-11453-8

1. Mohawk youth—Social life and customs—Juvenile literature.
2. Mohawk Indians—Social life and customs—Juvenile literature.
3. Akwesasne Indian Reserve (Québec and Ont.)—Social life and customs—
Juvenile literature. 4. Saint Regis Mohawk Indian Reservation (N.Y.)—
Social life and customs—Juvenile literature.
I. Poole, Stephen R. II. Title. III. Series: Gravelle, Karen. Growing up in America.
E99.M8G725 1997
971.4'34—dc21   97-10343   CIP
                                          AC

CONTENTS

ACKNOWLEDGMENTS

I'd like to thank Chantelle Francis, David Francis, and their families for all the help they gave me in writing this book. Of course, I would never have met them if it hadn't been for Mr. Irving Papineau, the former principal of Akwesasne Mohawk School. Many thanks, Mr. Papineau, for introducing me to such wonderful people! I'd also like to express my appreciation to others at the school, including Chantelle's teacher, Mrs. Karen Dixon; David's teacher, Mr. Steve Bradley; and Mr. Romaine Mitchell, the current principal.

I am also very grateful to Mrs. Mavis Etienne, of Oka, for the time and effort she spent in helping me to understand the confrontation that occurred there.

Finally, a special thanks to Mrs. Hilda Garcia of Akwesasne, a good friend whose support made doing this book possible.

K.G.

In many ways, people in the United States are very similar to one another. We all listen to the same music, watch the same movies and television programs, eat the same burgers, French fries, and pizza, and wear the same clothes.

But if you look closer, you'll see that Americans are different from each other too. Not only do we have traits that make each of us unique in-

dividuals, but we often have different cultural characteristics that identify us as belonging to a particular ethnic, religious, or racial group.

Generally, the longer a particular group of people live in this country and interact with other Americans, the more they become like everyone else. Thus, after a few generations, most immigrants retain relatively little of their original cultures.

However, some groups have been in this country for hundreds of years, yet have kept alive the cultures of their ancestors. In most ways, they live just like other Americans. But, at the same time, they have preserved their own special traditions, religious beliefs, music, foods, ways of talking, and sometimes even their own languages.

Many of these groups came from Europe or Africa, while others are Native Americans who have been here all along. But all have made important contributions to the way Americans live and to the common culture that we share.

I thought you might like to meet some children from these different cultures and learn about their lives, so I decided to write this series, *Growing Up in America*, to introduce them to you. You may have already heard of the Mohawk Indians,* or seen them portrayed in movies or on television. Since television and movies rarely present the Mohawk people as they really are, I wanted you to get to know some Mohawk children. Like other Native Americans, they have to work hard to hold on to their way of life. But since they value the special things that make them Mohawks, it is worth the effort.

There is a Mohawk reservation, the St. Regis Indian Reservation, in northern New York State, the state in which I live, so that seemed like a good place to start. I asked the principal of one of the reservation schools to introduce me to two children who would enjoy helping me write this book. He thought Chantelle Francis and her cousin, David Francis, would be perfect. I think you'll agree with me that he was right!

*Many Native people refer to themselves as Native Americans, while others call themselves Indians. Therefore, you will find both terms used in this book

CHANTELLE AND DAVID

It was a spring day long ago, before the coming of the white people. Two **Mohawk** hunters moved quietly through the forests near the St. Lawrence River, searching for signs of game. Suddenly, from behind a small hill came the sound of drumming. The hunters quickly crouched to the ground to avoid being seen. Others must be here too! Who could they be? Stealthily, the two men crept to the top of the hill and peered through the bushes.

"To their surprise, they saw a male **partridge** sitting on a log flapping its wings, making a sound like someone drumming," says ten-year-old Chantelle Francis, picking up the story. "Ever since then, we've called this place Akwesasne. That means, where the partridge drums its wings."

A male ruffed grouse, commonly called a partridge, drumming its wings

Chantelle, her ten-year-old cousin, David Francis, and their families are among the 9,000 Mohawk people who still live at Akwesasne, or the St. Regis Indian **Reservation**, as it is called in English. The Mohawk are the easternmost members of the **Iroquois Confederacy**. Originally, Mohawk lands extended from the St. Lawrence River in the north to the Mohawk River valley in central New York State. Although the territory in central New York was lost to white settlers two hundred years ago, Mohawk people still live in, and control, scattered communities in northern New York and southern Canada. Akwesasne is one of these communities.

THE LONGHOUSE

The Mohawk are an **Iroquois** nation. The Iroquois called themselves the Hodenesaune, or People of the Longhouse, after the type of homes in which they lived. As the name suggests, these dwellings were very long—between 50 and 100 feet (15 and 30 m) in length—and narrow. They were built of wooden poles covered with tree bark and had a door at the front and in the back. Some longhouses were decorated with intricate designs in red and black painted on the outside walls.

Inside, raised platforms lining the walls served as benches to sit on during the day and beds to sleep on at night. Fires were placed at intervals in the corridor in the middle for cooking and to provide light. The roof of the longhouse was rounded and had holes at various points to let smoke from the fires escape.

Depending on the size of the longhouse, up to twenty families, related through blood or marriage, might share a single home. Woven mats of bark or corn husks were used to divide family sections of the sleeping area, and to provide privacy. Possessions were stored on a second row of platforms above the beds or hung from pegs on the supporting poles.

The Iroquois had a clever answer to the problem of housing a growing family. Whenever a new marriage meant that more room was needed, the rear wall of the longhouse was removed, another section was added on, and the wall was put back in place.

The students at Chantelle and David's school made this mural of a longhouse out of bark, the same material their ancestors used to build their houses.

Chantelle giggles when she comes to the part of her story in which Jay gets squished.

Chantelle loves the story about the drumming partridge. In fact, she likes any good story, whether it's a traditional Mohawk tale or a new murder mystery. In Chantelle's fifth-grade class, the students read a lot of stories, and they write their own as well—usually with their friends as the main characters.

"My friend, Jay, killed me in his story," Chantelle says. "He had a rabid raccoon cough on me." Chantelle returned the favor in the next story she wrote. "Jay accidentally stepped in front of a shrinkilator machine that made him the size of an ant. Dori didn't see him and stepped on him. When Dori checked the bottoms of her shoes, there was Jay. Yuck!" she adds, laughing.

Chantelle and her classmates hold up their choices for the next book to be read. As usual, she votes for a Goosebumps book.

Although the Mohawk Nation is made up of reservations in both the United States and Canada, Akwesasne is the only one that actually straddles the border. This can make going to school—as well as many other things—very complicated.

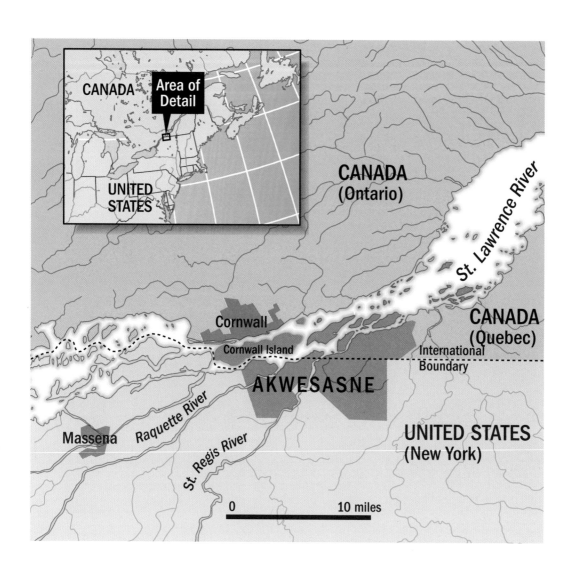

WHERE IS AKWESASNE?

Akwesasne, or the St. Regis Indian Reservation, is on the St. Lawrence River, straddling the border between the United States and Canada. The part of the reservation that is on the U.S. side is in the state of New York. This portion is approximately 6 miles square (15.5 sq. km). The part that is on the Canadian side is divided between two provinces, Quebec and Ontario. (A Canadian province is similar to a state in the U.S.) The total territory on the Canadian side is roughly the same size as the U.S. section of the reservation.

In addition to the territory on the mainland, forty-nine islands in the St. Lawrence River are also part of the Canadian side of Akwesasne. These islands are scattered over about 60

Three beautiful rivers run through Akwesasne.

(96.6 km) miles from upstream to downstream. The largest is Cornwall Island. That's where Chantelle and David live. Their school is on Cornwall Island too.

There are two towns in Akwesasne, Hogansburg and St. Regis Village. There's also a lot of water. Besides the St. Lawrence River, two smaller rivers run through the mainland. One is the St. Regis River and the other is the Raquette River. With all these rivers, there's plenty of opportunity for fishing and swimming.

Fishing is a popular activity on the St. Regis River.

There are four elementary schools on the reservation, three on the Canadian side and one on the American side. There is also a public school just outside the reservation in Hogansburg, New York, which some Mohawk children attend. Because of the unique location of Akwesasne, children on the reservation can go to school on either side of the border, regardless of which country they live in. Most children go to the school that's closest to their home. The Akwesasne Mohawk School is on Cornwall Island in Canada, where David and Chantelle both live, so that's the one they attend.

Chantelle and David are very proud of their school. They take the same subjects as other Canadian children, and they also study the Mohawk language and culture.

Each morning, classes begin with a prayer of thanksgiving spoken in Mohawk. At

Each classroom door has a plaque illustrating something that is important in Mohawk culture. The one on David's door shows corn, squash, and beans—traditional Mohawk foods. The colored signs say autumn, in Mohawk.

15

David and Cory and Matt, Andrew, and Brandon work on solving algebra problems.

the end of the day, the same prayer is said again. Since the Mohawk people traditionally use this prayer to begin and end any meeting or function, it's important for children to know it well.

Like the children in Chantelle's class, the students in David's fourth-grade class work hard. He and four other boys have already finished their fourth-grade math book, so they've started learning algebra. In addition to enjoying math, David also likes to work on the computer.

David's teacher is very good at thinking of ways to make learning fun. He decided that if the students were going to insult each other, they should learn some new and more interesting names to use. So, he gave them lists of old-

Steve, David's teacher, writes some of the insults on the board, while the class tries to think of ones that are even better.

fashioned words from Shakespeare, the sixteenth-century English writer who was a champion at inventing nasty names. After coming up with a particularly good insult, the children draw a picture to illustrate it.

SHAKESPEAREAN INSULTS

You can learn to insult your friends in Shakespearean English too. These are only a few of the words David and his classmates use, but they're enough to give you a start.

Pick one word from each column. Then place the word, "Thou," in front and hurl your insult at someone who deserves it.

Column 1	Column 2	Column 3
beslubbering	bat-fowling	bladder
craven	beetle-headed	boar-pig
fawning	fat-kidneyed	flap-dragon
fobbing	fen-sucked	foot-licker
frothy	fly-bitten	horn-beast
loggerheaded	full-gorged	hugger-mugger
mammering	hasty-witted	maggot-pie
mewling	milk-livered	malt-worm
puking	motley-minded	moldwarp
reeky	pox-marked	pignut
ruttish	rump-fed	ratsbane
tottering	swag-bellied	strumpet
yeasty	toad-spotted	wagtail

R ecently, the students of Akwesasne Mohawk School had a jump-rope campaign to raise money to enlarge their building. They asked friends, family members, and neighbors to sponsor them by making a donation. In return, they promised to jump rope for an entire afternoon.

Having fun while raising money at the same time.

As you can imagine, jumping rope for that long wasn't easy. There were a lot of tangled ropes and tired students by the end of the day, but everyone thought it was well worth it.

Although English is spoken by everyone in Akwesasne, about a third of the people—many of them elderly individuals—

Chantelle and her friend find it hard not to laugh when they keep stepping on the rope.

also speak Mohawk. For years, students were prohibited from speaking any Native American language in Canadian and American public schools. Thus, most people the age of David's and Chantelle's parents did not learn to speak their own language. As a result, Mohawk was in danger of dying out.

Since then, the community has made a big effort to help young people learn Mohawk as well as English. Mohawk is taught in reservation schools on both sides of the border, and 10 to 15 percent of the children use only Mohawk names.

As Chantelle's mother says, "We have a **prophecy** among our people that the day will come when the children will be

Students put their Mohawk names on their lockers.

teaching us our language. And that's what's happening here. Chantelle and her sister come home from school and teach me the opening prayer and other things."

Even though the children receive Mohawk lessons in school, Chantelle's parents don't think this is enough. Chantelle agrees. "We get only forty-five minutes of Mohawk," she says. "And the teacher goes so fast."

Like most girls, Chantelle and her friends like to hang out and talk during recess.

So, when Chantelle's younger sister, Chelsea, was old enough to begin kindergarten, her parents enrolled her in the Freedom School. Here, the children take the same subjects as students in the regular public school, but all the classes are taught in Mohawk. Chelsea uses only her Mohawk name, Okiokwinon, in school. The students learn English too, because they hear it all the time outside of school. But they don't start to read and write English in class until the sixth grade.

At the Freedom School, everyone, regardless of age, starts in kindergarten unless he or she is already fluent in Mohawk. Since Chantelle is a little old to start school there now, she tries

Chantelle's younger sister, left, goes to the Freedom School. Her baby sister and brother also get a lot of exposure to the Mohawk language because their sitter speaks it to them all the time.

to practice speaking Mohawk in other ways. "The babysitter speaks Mohawk to me lots of times," she says. "If I don't understand, I just ask what she said and she tells me."

After-school sports are important for most boys and girls on the reservation. David loves just about any sport, but his favorite is lacrosse, a game that originated with Native American people.

Chantelle spends a lot of her after-school time with her puppies.

Lacrosse has been called the fastest game on two feet, and it can be a rough-and-tumble sport. Two teams play against each other, each trying to get the ball into its own goal. Players run down the field, or court, carrying the ball in a webbed pocket at the end of a stick. They can pass the ball to each other, but they must throw and catch it with their sticks. It takes a lot of skill to keep the ball from falling out of the pocket, especially when other players shove you or hit your stick with theirs.

Lacrosse is a very old game. Historically, it was played by many Native American nations for fun, physical fitness, and spiritual development. Often, there were as many as one hundred players on each team, all pushing and shoving to get the ball. There was no time limit, and the two teams played until one team managed to score three goals, even if that meant playing for several days.

Because it was a gift from the Creator to the people, playing lacrosse was a way of giving thanks to God. Lacrosse was also played to honor individuals and to add spiritual power to efforts to heal the sick. Sometimes, lacrosse was used to settle important disagreements between tribes. In this case, the team that won the game also won the dispute.

David, in blue, and an opponent battle for the ball at the start of a lacrosse game.

DREAMCATCHERS

Dreamcatchers were originally made by the Plains Indians, who believe that the air is filled with both good and bad dreams. Traditionally, dreamcatchers such as the one pictured below were hung in the **tipi** or **lodge** or on a baby's cradleboard. Today, they are hung everywhere, but especially in the bedroom. The good dreams are able to pass through the center hole to a sleeping person. But the bad dreams are trapped in the woven web, where they perish in the light of dawn.

The popularity of dreamcatchers has spread to Native American communities throughout the United States and among many non-Indian people as well. Iroquois craftspeople have long been known for their intricate bead and quill work, so it is no surprise that they can make beautiful dreamcatchers too. In addition to creating dreamcatchers for themselves, some people at Akwesasne also make them for sale outside the community as a way of earning money.

Dreamcatchers are beautiful wherever they are placed.

Although lacrosse was played by many Indian nations, it has become identified with the Iroquois, particularly the Mohawk. Even before the arrival of Europeans, competitions between tribes had become popular among the different Mohawk villages. In the late 1600s and early 1700s, these contests were witnessed by colonial settlers, and the game began to catch on with them as well.

Akwesasne has a special place in the history of lacrosse. For many years, lacrosse sticks produced by the Mohawk factory on Cornwall Island were considered the finest in the world. They were so popular that 97 percent of the lacrosse sticks used throughout the world were made there. Unfortunately, the factory burned down, and the land is now used for other purposes.

As the referee, David's father (in black) reminds each team of the rules.

Although his father is refereeing this game, David's team doesn't get any special breaks.

Today, the new athletic building on Cornwall Island is home to both juvenile and adult lacrosse teams. David plays in the novice league, his sixteen-year-old brother, Guy, is in the intermediate league, and his father occasionally plays in the old-timers' league. David's dad is also one of the referees, while his mom provides support from the bleachers.

With such a long tradition of playing lacrosse, it's no surprise that players from Akwesasne are very good. This year, David's team took second place in the entire province of Ontario, which is equivalent to coming in second in a state championship in the U.S. David was especially happy because he scored four goals in the playoffs!

THE IROQUOIS CONFEDERACY

It was a bleak and bloody period sometime between A.D. 1350 and 1600 in what is now upstate New York. Endless wars and murderous feuds raged among the five Iroquois nations that inhabited this area, threatening to destroy them all.

Into the midst of this desperate situation came a Huron named Deganawida, the Peacemaker. Together with Hiawatha, an Onondaga exile living among the Mohawk, he persuaded the warring nations to join in a Great Peace. On the shores of Onondaga Lake, the Peacemaker planted the Tree of Peace, a white pine under which the Five Nations buried their weapons.

Out of the Great Peace came the Iroquois Confederacy, consisting of the Mohawk, the Oneida, the Onondaga,

The Tree of Peace, where the five Iroquois Nations buried their weapons, is pictured throughout Akwesasne. This mural is from David and Chantelle's school.

the Seneca, and the Cayuga. In 1722, they were joined by the Tuscarora, who had migrated north after being pushed out of North Carolina by white settlers.

As a result of their own strength and their alliances with other Native American nations, the Iroquois Confederacy became a major political and military power in colonial America. Without the Confederacy's help, the British would have been unable to defeat the French in the Colonial Wars for control of the American Northeast.

The Iroquois made another very important contribution to the shaping of what is now the United States. Their government—six separate nations united in a strong democratic union—inspired Benjamin Franklin and others of the Continental Congress, who used the Iroquois Confederacy as a model for uniting the thirteen independent colonies into a federation.

Chantelle would like to play lacrosse, but her mother feels this is not a sport for girls. "I keep telling Chantelle that she's not supposed to play," her mother says. "The Creator didn't give lacrosse to the women, he gave it to the men."

In the past, lacrosse was a male game. Players were not supposed to touch a woman for seven days before a game and seven days after. If a woman even touched a player's stick before the game, it would not be used.

Many non-Native Americans thought this meant that Indians felt women were somehow dirty or inferior. Actually, the reverse was the case. It was believed that the special strength of

Chantelle is wearing her favorite Mohawk dress. She holds a beaded bag, a horn rattle used in Mohawk dances, and a rabbit skin. The right photograph shows traditional Mohawk men's clothing.

women could overcome and weaken a player. Even today, many Mohawks still feel that women have powers that are the opposite of those men need and, therefore, the two should not be mixed.

Among the Iroquois nations, women have always held positions of authority. Although **chiefs** are male, they must be nominated and approved by the women. The women can also dismiss the chief if they feel he isn't doing a good job. This is still true in the traditional government of the Six Nations.

In the old days, women also controlled the food supply. It

was the job of men to protect the community, and warriors who were particularly courageous in battle were highly respected. Since waging war was a primary way for a man to gain honor, warriors were often eager to fight. But the women had to agree that a war was necessary. If they disagreed, they could stop the men from going by refusing to give them food for the journey. That way, any war that was fought had the support and approval of the entire community.

The choosing of traditional leaders, such as Chief, **Faithkeeper**, and **Clan Mother**, is very important, particularly because these are lifetime positions. "Right now, we're looking for people to fill positions in the clan," Chantelle's mother says, "and we can't find the perfect Chief. We have to have someone who knows the language, so that narrows the choice down quite a bit. The person has to be responsible—not drinking or doing drugs or being abusive—and that means a lot of background checking. We have to ask, 'How was he when he was younger? Do you know how he is now? Does he look out for other people?'"

CLANS

Most Native American nations were originally organized into clans. A clan is a group of people who are descended from a common ancestor. Because they are related, members of a clan cannot marry each other but must choose husbands and wives from other clans. In some tribes, children become part of their mother's clan, while in others, they join their father's clan.

This carved plaque at the front of the Mohawk Assembly of God church shows the three Mohawk clans—the bear, wolf, and turtle.

Among the Iroquois, including the Mohawk, children inherit the clan of their mother. David's mother is a turtle and his father is a wolf, so David and his brother, Guy, are both part of the turtle clan. Chantelle and her brother and sisters are part of their mother's clan, the turtle. Their father is a snipe.

Clans traditionally played a central role in the lives of American Indians. Clan members had special obligations to each other and shared ceremonial responsibilities, privileges, and restrictions. Today, clans have lost much of their importance in some Indian nations, but not among the Mohawk. Although some Mohawks no longer feel bound to marry according to clan rules, others do. And clan membership is still very important in Akwesasne.

There are nine clans among the original Five Nations of the Iroquois Confederacy. The Mohawk and the Oneida are each made up of the same three clans—the wolf, bear, and turtle. The Cayuga and the Seneca are also composed of the wolf, bear, and turtle clans. But in addition, some of the Cayuga are members of the deer and the heron clans, while some of the Seneca belong to the snipe and the hawk clans. The Onondaga clans are the wolf, turtle, deer, beaver, and eel.

"Even when we choose a person to represent us, the women of the other clans may look at him and say, 'We don't accept him.' If we really want him, we have to bring him up again and argue for him."

The position of Clan Mother is very important in traditional Mohawk society. One of her many duties is to help in choosing each baby's Mohawk name. Since a baby must have a name from the moment it comes into the world, a name is picked before the child is born. Both a boy's name and a girl's name are chosen, so the name is waiting for the baby. Chantelle's Mohawk name is Watewanahawetha, which means "within she carries her voice." David's is Tawit (pronounced Dah-wee) Wennisirio. His name means "a nice guy."

"Nobody else has my name in the Mohawk Nation," Chantelle explains. "And no one else can have it until I die. That's why we don't need Mohawk last names, because nobody else who is living has your same name."

"Your Mohawk name is supposed to be a name that has been in your family for generations," Chantelle's mother adds. "But along the way, some names weren't carried on in the same family line, so they were given back into the clan pot."

It's the Clan Mother's responsibility to know all the names that belong to the clan and to remember which ones are in use by living people. She discusses the available names with the mother and guides her in choosing the best name for the baby.

Although traditional leaders, such as Chief, Faithkeeper, and Clan Mother, are very influential in the community, the traditional government is only one of three governments on Akwesasne. There are two elected tribal governments as well, one on the American side and one on the Canadian side.

The Mohawk are considered an independent nation, separate from both the United States and Canada. Thus, state, provincial, and federal governments do not have legal authority on the reservation. This means, for example, that in the U.S. portion of Akwesasne, federal and state agencies such as the FBI, the New York State Department of Taxation, and the Internal Revenue Service are not allowed. Law and order is maintained by the St. Regis Mohawk Tribal Police, so New York

Signs on the roads leading into Akwesasne remind state and federal agencies that they are not permitted to enter the reservation.

State police and county sheriffs are neither needed nor welcome.

The people of Akwesasne have good reason to be distrustful of state, provincial, and federal governments. Like other Native Americans, they've learned the hard way never to let down their guard in the effort to maintain their independence and territory. Once rights or land have been lost, it can be very difficult, if not impossible, to get them back.

Only a few years ago, a town in Quebec attempted to take over the Mohawk burial ground at Oka, a nearby reservation, in order to extend the town golf course. The people of Oka responded by camping on the land to stop construction. The Quebec provincial police attacked the campers—including the women and children—with tear gas, concussion grenades, and

Some Mohawk businesses take a humorous look at past confrontations between Native people and the U.S. government.

bullets. Other Mohawks rushed in to defend their people, and an armed confrontation resulted between Mohawks, on one side, and the Quebec provincial police and the Canadian army, on the other. The siege lasted for weeks, ending only when the government agreed to negotiate in good faith with the Mohawks.

Sadly, as soon as the Mohawks laid down their guns, the government went back on its word. Many protesters were beaten and arrested when they came out from behind the barricades, and it took two years before they were cleared by the courts. But the Mohawks of Oka were successful in saving their land.

Sometimes, pressures from outside can be easier to

Large banners on buildings in Akwesasne remind people of the struggle at Oka.

handle than internal disputes. A few years ago, the residents of Akwesasne split over the question of whether or not to permit gambling on the reservation. Fighting broke out and one of David's uncles was attacked and killed. This was a very difficult time for David's family, and the entire community still looks back on this period of conflict with great sadness.

Since then, however, the people of Akwesasne have worked hard to pull together and go forward. One sign of this

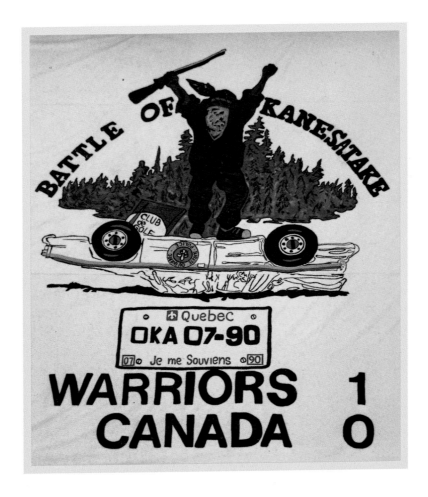

effort is the progress that has been made in improving the quality of life on the reservation.

New homes can be seen everywhere. Many of them are being constructed by the Mohawk Housing Authority, but David's mom and dad have been building theirs themselves. This way, it will be exactly the way they want. There's a lot more room in the new place for David, his brother, Guy, his mom and dad, and David's three dogs.

David sits on the porch of his new house with his dogs. Rambo (left) guards David's entire street. Caesar (middle) is still a puppy. Dakota (right) is nicknamed Mutley. He was a stray that David fed with a baby bottle.

In addition to expansions of both Akwesasne Mohawk School and the St. Regis Mohawk School, the reservation also has a new health complex, where both David's mother and Chantelle's mother work.

The words over the entrance of the new Health Complex say "Place of Good Medicine," in Mohawk.

KANONHKWA'TSHERI:IO

David's mother and uncle work together in their family's pharmacy in the health complex. Chantelle's mother (above) works downstairs in the substance abuse program.

The inside of David's house is very modern, but many of the things in it are likely to be found only in a Native American home. These baskets, woven in traditional Mohawk style, were made by members of David's family. The basket in the small picture has served as both a laundry basket and a bed for a baby.

WALKING IN THE SKY

Perched high above a river building a bridge, or suspended forty to fifty floors above city streets constructing a skyscraper are extremely dangerous places to earn a living. Men who want to work on high steel, as these bridges and buildings are called, are few, and men who can do it well are even rarer. The workers must conquer their fear of falling, and the noise from riveting often makes them feel sick and dizzy.

Unlike other construction workers, Mohawk men have become famous throughout the world for their ability to work effortlessly in the sky. As a bridge official commented long ago, "These Indians…do not have any fear of heights. They're as agile as goats. They can walk a narrow beam high up in the air with nothing below them, and it doesn't mean any more to them than walking on solid ground. Putting riveting tools in their hands is like putting ham with eggs. They're natural-born bridgemen."

Needless to say, men who can do this type of work are well-paid. However, while earning a good living is an important part of the job for Mohawk men, this isn't the only reason why they become high-steel workers. Walking in the sky also allows them to test their courage and abilities in the face of danger as their ancestors did, and to prove themselves as Mohawk men.

Both David's father, Stanley, and Chantelle's father, John, have been high-steel workers. David's dad works on the bridge between the U.S. and Canada. Chantelle's father is a welder at several locations.

It's only a short distance from the health complex to David's grandfather's farm where his mom keeps her horse, Cheyenne. "Cheyenne isn't trained yet, so we can't ride her," David explains. "Right now, we're just trying to get her used to being around people." Every morning before school, David and his mom feed Cheyenne, clean her stall, and let her out in the pasture.

As David's mom gets ready to let Cheyenne out of her stall, David feeds her an apple. He's careful to keep his hand flat so Cheyenne doesn't mistake his fingers for part of the fruit.

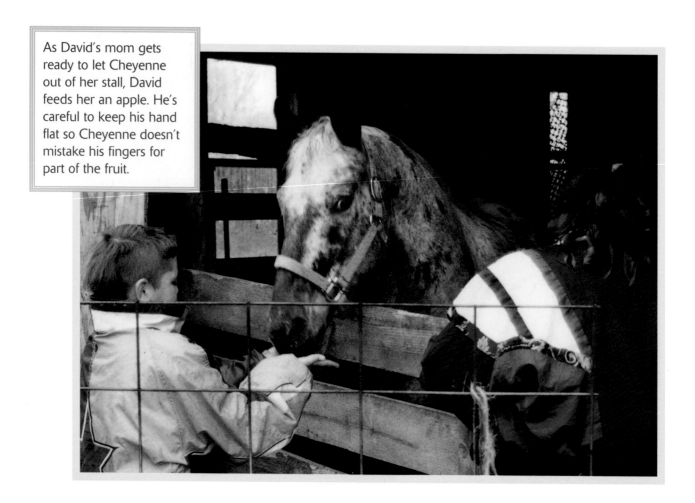

While Cheyenne is outdoors, David cleans the barn. But first, he has to separate two fighting turkeys who keep getting in his way.

Although David and his family live in the Canadian portion of Akwesasne, his grandfather's farm is on the American side. "David and Guy will inherit this land after my father," his mom explains. "We wanted to be sure that the boys have land in both Canada and the U.S., so they will always have a place, no matter which country they decide to live in."

David and his mom walk around the pasture, trying to get Cheyenne to follow them.

David coaxes Cheyenne to come to him by offering her some grass.

As they grow up, David, Chantelle, and the other children in Akwesasne must decide not only where they want to live, but how they want to live—which aspects of the mainstream culture they wish to adopt and which Mohawk cultural values and traditions they wish to keep. For some people, retaining their Mohawk culture means working hard to keep the Mohawk language alive. For others, it means returning to the spiritual beliefs and practices of their ancestors or incorporating these beliefs into Christianity. For many, it involves remaining connected to Mother Earth and the gifts of the Creator.

RELIGION

The Iroquois believed in many spirit forces, all created by a supreme being, the Creator. These forces were everywhere—in the wind, thunder, Sun, Moon, stars, plants, animals, and, of course, people. They controlled the weather and the lives of all living things.

Honoring and living in harmony with these spirit forces was very important. Because the forces of the Creator were present in everything, human actions, such as the cutting down of a tree for a canoe or the killing of an animal for food, all had spiritual significance. Thus, for the Iroquois, religion was not separate from the rest of their lives but a part of everything they did.

Each year, the Iroquois held a number of religious cere-

Now, as in the past, traditional religious ceremonies are held in a special longhouse.

monies which were conducted in a special longhouse. The most important of these was midwinter, or New Year. Ceremonial dances, an important form of prayer for all Native Americans, were a big part of these events. In addition to dancing, they feasted, played games, made speeches, and gave thanks to the spirits of The Three Sisters—corn, beans, and squash.

In the early 1600s, the French colonizers brought with

them Catholic missionaries whose purpose was to convert as many Native Americans as possible. Over the next several hundred years, many Mohawks became Catholics. More recently, others have become Protestant. Today, in addition to the Catholic church in Akwesasne, there is a Methodist church, the Assembly of God, and the Church of Christ.

The traditional religion of the Mohawk, the Longhouse, is far from dead. In fact, more and more people are returning to the Longhouse. Most do not refer to the Longhouse as a religion, however. As they point out, it has always been much more than that. It's an entire way of life. David's family was brought up Catholic, but his brother, Guy, and his uncle have returned to the Longhouse. Chantelle's family are all members of the Longhouse.

For Chantelle, preserving traditional Mohawk songs and dances is very important. "Each dance has a different meaning," she explains. "In the raccoon dance, we're giving thanks to the raccoons. We also have the fishing dance and the rabbit dance, where you dance like a rabbit." In addition to dances like these, which are spiritual, other dances, like the duck dance, are done more for fun.

Mohawk dancing is different from the dances of many Native Americans in the West. "In a lot of western tribes, they dance clockwise. We go counterclockwise," Chantelle says. "Also, we use **rattles** and a **water drum**. They use a big drum, and they never use rattles with it."

Catholics especially honor Kateri Tekakwitha, a Mohawk saint.

The biggest difference between Mohawk dancing and **powwow**, or fancy dancing from the western groups, is that Mohawk singing and dancing isn't very competitive. "That's not the Iroquois way," Chantelle's mother explains. "We don't do powwows—that's not our thing. But we've had people who've gone to powwows and think the dancing and singing are pretty neat, so they bring it back. But it's really new here."

WAMPUM

Wampum are white and purple beads made from the shells of marine clams, whelks, and periwinkles. Because of the difficult work involved in grinding the shells into a cylindrical shape, wampum beads are very valuable.

Wampum was used in documenting treaties, laws, pacts, and marriage contracts. The beads were woven into a belt with a special design that symbolized the terms of the agreement. Each party to the agreement received an identical wampum belt as a record of the pledge made. Wampum belts were also carried by tribal ambassadors as proof of their credentials.

Each nation of the Iroquois has its own special strings of wampum. When speakers at an Iroquois council address the council, they hold the wampum strings in their hands. The Mohawk Nation's wampum is six strings tied together, with two purple beads for every one white bead.

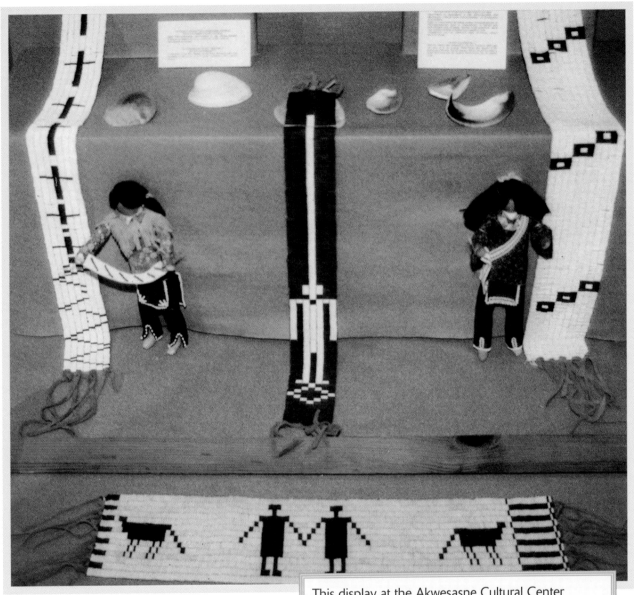

This display at the Akwesasne Cultural Center shows several different wampum belts and the types of shells used to make them. Similar wampum belts were used in recording the Great Peace between the Five Iroquois Nations.

One aspect of Mohawk culture that almost everyone participates in is eating the traditional foods that their ancestors prepared long ago. But at first glance, you might not think of these items as Native American. That's because the rest of us have been eating Native American food for so long that we've forgotten where it came from in the first place. For example, no one would be eating pizza, French fries, or popcorn today, if Native Americans hadn't introduced European settlers to tomatoes, potatoes, and corn.

Corn, beans, and squash, called The Three Sisters, have always been important to the Iroquois people. These foods are still big favorites today. "When our pen pals from Ottawa came to visit my class," David says, "we gave them Mohawk food—corn soup, hash, and strawberry juice."

"Corn soup is made of white corn, yellow corn, string beans, lima beans, kidney beans, carrots, and anything else you've grown in your garden," Chantelle explains. "It also has venison or some other meat."

Chantelle thinks corn soup is delicious, but she likes corn mush even more. To make this dish, dried white corn is cooked in ashes, then washed. This process is repeated several times until the corn is just right. Since this takes a lot of time, Chantelle's mother sometimes buys corn that is already prepared.

The rest is easy, and Chantelle can finish making corn mush by herself in just a few minutes. First, she takes the corn and puts it in a blender. Then she mixes the blended corn with maple syrup and cooks it in a frying pan.

Strawberries have always had a special place among the Iroquois. As Awehai, the ancestor of the Iroquois people, was

Chantelle takes washed corn from the container on the left and runs it through the blender. After frying it, Chantelle samples her corn mush and decides it's very good.

falling from the Sky World into this world, she grabbed a strawberry plant with one hand and tobacco leaves with the other. The strawberry ceremony, held each spring, is to thank the strawberry for its gift of medicine and food.

But the most important Mohawk ceremony is New Year, or midwinter. The Mohawk New Year occurs near the middle of winter, rather than on December 31. There are seven days of thanksgiving, prayer, and feasting. Afterwards, the Mohawk play a sacred game. "The Creator enjoys seeing his people play after days of working and praying," Chantelle's mother says. "That's why he gave this game to us."

"It's called the peach stone game," Chantelle explains. "There's a big bowl with peach pits in it. To play, you have to contribute something of great value to you. It doesn't have to be expensive—but it should be something that means a lot to you."

Sometimes, artists put in a painting they have done, or basketweavers contribute a basket. An especially good lacrosse player may put in a lacrosse stick. It's appropriate to use these items in this game because artistic talent and skill at lacrosse are gifts from the Creator. But jewelry or shiny objects are never included. Trivial things such as these have no survival or spiritual value, so they are not important enough to be contributed.

"You take a chance because you could lose it," Chantelle adds. "Last year, I put in my moccasins."

The Longhouse is divided into two sides according to clan. Each side tries to match the things put in by the other side. Since Chantelle contributed moccasins, someone from the other side put in a pair of moccasins too.

The peach stones have been blackened on one side. "You toss the bowl up and count how many stones have flipped,"

Chantelle contributed her treasured moccasins to the peach stone game.

Chantelle continues. "Each side gets beans to keep score. Whichever side runs out of their beans first loses." Chantelle's side won, so she got to keep the other pair of moccasins in addition to her own.

But the peach stone game is not just a simple game of chance. It has a very important spiritual meaning too. "If you lose something, it's not really lost," Chantelle says. "Because when you pass on from this world to the next world, it will be waiting for you."

Only a few decades ago, it appeared that the Mohawk culture might be in danger of fading away. But, as in the peach stone game, what may have appeared to be lost was not really gone. Instead, the things that the Mohawk people treasure— their language, values, and traditions—are alive, well, and growing stronger. Chantelle, David, and the other children of Akwesasne are proof of that.

GLOSSARY

Chief—Each clan has a chief who represents the clan at meetings. In traditional Iroquois society, the chief is always a man, although women are largely responsible for choosing him. A chief's actions must always be for the good of the people—otherwise, he will be removed from office.

Clan—A group of people who are descended from a common ancestor.

Clan Mother—A very important position in Iroquois society. Among other things, she is responsible for keeping track of the names that belong to the Clan and helps women choose the names for their babies.

Faithkeeper—The Faithkeeper makes sure that all the ceremonies are done correctly and at the right time of year. The Faithkeeper can be a man or a woman.

Iroquois—A group of Native American nations living in New York State and Canada who have similar languages and cultures.

Iroquois Confederacy—or The League of Six Nations. The Mohawk, Onondaga, Seneca, Oneida, Cayuga, and Tuscarora nations, who are joined in an alliance.

Lodge—One of a variety of homes used by Native Americans. Unlike tipis, lodges were not picked up and moved from one place to another.

Mohawk—A Native American nation living in northern New York State and nearby areas of Canada.

Partridge—A common name for the ruffed grouse, a medium-sized bird. Male partridges attract females by beating their wings. This is what the early Mohawk hunters at Akwesasne saw.

Powwow—A large gathering of Native people that lasts several days. It is a chance for Indians of different nations to meet each other, participate in cultural activities, and honor the Creator by singing, drumming, and dancing.

Prophecy—A prediction of a future event.

Rattle—An instrument consisting of seeds, beads, or other small objects inside a hollow container, such as a gourd. When shaken, the objects make a noise. Mohawk rattles are usually a horn or hoof filled with beads, BBs, or ball bearings.

Reservation—Land area set aside for use by a particular group of Indians.

Tipi—A tentlike home used by nomadic Indians of the Great Plains. A tipi consists of poles arranged in a circle and tied together at the top. The pole framework is covered with leather hides. Tipis are light, and can easily be put up and taken down, so they are perfect for people who more from place to place.

Water drum—A drum filled with water. It makes a softer "ping" sound than the booming of powwow drums.

MORE ABOUT THE MOHAWK AND OTHER IROQUOIS NATIONS

BOOKS

Picture Books

Giving Thanks: A Native American Good Morning. By Chief Jake Swamp, Mohawk Nation (Lee and Low Books, 1995).

> Chief Swamp has taken the short version of the Mohawk Thanksgiving Prayer used to open each day and presented it in English. The Mohawk words are given at the end of the book.

Non-Fiction

The Iroquois. By Craig A. Doherty and Katherine M. Doherty (Franklin Watts, 1989).

> This book tells what life was like among the Iroquois before the arrival of European settlers. It includes plenty of color illustrations to help you get an idea of how things actually looked.

People of the Longhouse: How the Iroquois Tribes Lived. By Jillian and Robin Ridington (Firefly Books, 1982).

> Like the book above, *People of the Longhouse* describes life among the Iroquois before the Europeans arrived. In addition, it includes neighboring nations that also spoke Iroquois, such as the Huron, the Tobacco, the Neutral, and the Erie Indians. The many big black-and-white drawings provide a lot of details that other books don't.

US Kids History: Book of the American Indians. By Marlene Smith-Baranzini and Howard Egger-Bovet (Little Brown and Company, 1994).

> This book combines history, traditional legends, stories, and illustrations to tell you about North American Indians from the Pacific to the Atlantic coasts.

North American Indians. By Herman J. Viola (Crown Publishers, 1996).

This book uses facts, vivid color photographs, and short essays by modern-day Native Americans to tell you about life—both past and present—in the different Indian nations.

Scholastic Encyclopedia of the North American Indian. By James Ciment (with Ronald LaFrance) (Scholastic, 1996).

This book is organized alphabetically like an encyclopedia. You can look up different Native American nations, famous historical and present-day Indians, objects used in Native American life, and just about anything else you'd like to know on the topic. There are also lots of pictures and photographs.

Soaring Spirits: Conversations with Native American Teens. By Karen Gravelle (Franklin Watts, 1995).

Some of you who are a little older might like to know what it's like to be a teenager in Akwesasne and how that compares with being a teen on other reservations. In *Soaring Spirits*, seventeen Native American teenagers from the Mohawk, Ojibway, Cherokee, Shinnecock, Quinault, and Pueblo nations talk about their lives.

MOVIES

The Last of the Mohicans

Although *The Last of the Mohicans* is primarily about white colonists, two Mohican Indians, and a Huron warrior, the movie illustrates several things discussed in this book. The story takes place in 1757 in what was then Mohawk territory, and it will give you an idea of what it was like to be a colonist or a Native American caught in the war between the French and the British. If you listen carefully, you'll hear why the Mohawk decided to side with England. You can also see the wampum belt that Hawkeye, a white adopted son of the Mohicans, wears across his chest at all times. He uses this wampum belt to give his words added importance when he asks a Huron chief to spare the lives of two white women. Finally, there's a brief scene of a lacrosse game between the Indians and the colonists.

INDEX